D0427936

God Breathes
On Blended Families

A Testimony of the Becnel Family

Moe & Paige Becnel

Published by Healing Place Productions, Inc.
Baton Rouge, Louisiana 70809

About the Authors

Moe and Paige Becnel are natives of New Orleans, Louisiana and have resided in Baton Rouge, Louisiana since 1994.

Moe has a Bachelor of Science degree in electrical engineering and has worked in marketing and customer service for 26 years at a local electric utility.

Paige has 18 years combined education and work experience in the medical field, and Paige left the medical field in 1998 to take a staff position at Trinity Christian Center. Moe and Paige met in a Christian singles ministry in 1987 and were married in 1989, blending a family of five children. They have taught several Bible studies over the years and have had a heart for missionaries for 12 years. Moe and Paige have also experienced the struggles, failures, and eventual victory of blending a family together. God Breathes on Blended Families is the story of their blended family coming together in fullness.

Moe and Paige are members of Trinity Christian Center in Baton Rouge, and serve as Pastors of a vibrant TGIS (Thank God I'm Single) ministry under Senior Pastors Dino & DeLynn Rizzo. The vision of Trinity Christian Center is to be "A Healing Place for A Hurting World," and the TGIS ministry has been a place of healing, hope, and restoration for many frustrated and struggling single people and single parents. This Singles ministry has played a big part in the explosive growth of the church.

From the hands-on pastoring of the TGIS ministry at Trinity, to the planting of seeds in other churches for such a ministry, to the spreading of resources across the country and world for blended family support groups, the Becnels and their 5 wonderful children have been raised up for this time to take the message of hope, healing, and restoration to a hurting world.

Dino & DeLynn Rizzo
Sr. Pastors of Trinity Christian Center
Executive Producers, Healing Place Productions, Inc.

To contact the authors:

Moe & Paige Becnel
Phone: 225-753-2273
Fax: 225-753-7175
Email: info@healingplacechurch.org

Scripture taken from the HOLY BIBLE, NEW INTERNATIONAL VERSION®, NIV®
Copyright© 1973, 1978, 1984 by International Bible Society.
Used by permission of Zondervan Publishing House.
All rights reserved.

"MY LONG-DISTANCE LIFE" by Nick Sheff
From Newsweek, [2/15/99, Pg.16]
All rights reserved.
Reprinted by permission.

BREATHE ON ME by LUCY FISHER
©1997 Lucy Fisher/ Hillsongs Publishing(adm. in U.S. and Canada by Integrity's
Hosanna! Music)/ASCAP
All rights reserved. International copyright secured.
Used by permission.
c/o Integrity Music, Inc., 1000 Cody Road, Mobile, AL 36695

GOD BREATHES ON BLENDED FAMILIES
Copyright© 2000 by Moe Becnel/ Paige Becnel

All rights reserved, including the right to reproduce this book or portions thereof in any
form whatsoever, without the written permission of the Authors and Publisher.

Library of Congress Cataloging-in-Publication Data

ISBN: 0-9678680-0-9

Published by Healing Place Productions, Inc., 19202 Highland Road, Baton Rouge,
Louisiana 70809

Edited by Marlo Kirkpatrick, Marlo Writes

Cover design by Jimmy Cook, Baton Rouge, Louisiana

Printed in the United States of America.

Dedicated with all our love to all of our children

Melanie Becnel Broga
Jonathan Broga
Nicole Morriz Duplechain
Brad Duplechain
Jordan Becnel
Kristen Morriz
Jessica Becnel

Table of Contents

Our Definition of A Blended Family

Any marriage in which at least one of the spouses becomes a stepparent (new parent), regardless of the age of the children.

Other Definitions (Defined for the purpose of this book)

Natural parent – the maternal or paternal biological parent

Natural child or children – your biological child or children

New parent – stepparent; the spouse who gains a child or
children through marriage

New child or children – stepchild or stepchildren; child or
children gained through marriage;
your spouse's natural child or children

Extended parents – parents of both spouses

Extended family – parents, brothers, sisters, grandparents, aunts,
uncles and friends of both spouses

Former spouse – more commonly referred to as ex spouse,
or "ex"

Except for clarification, we purposely avoid using the words "stepparent," "ex-spouse" or "ex" in the text of this book.

The primary objective of a blended family is to establish a loving, caring relationship among everyone involved. The terms "stepmother," "stepfather," "stepbrother," "stepsister," etc. put the new parent and siblings in a different category than the natural parent and siblings. We believe the use of these terms puts the new relationships within the home in a lower category, and is a form of division within the home.

Prologue

On July 1, 1997, we celebrated our eighth wedding anniversary. As an anniversary surprise, our five children presented us with a video they had spent more than two months producing.

Titled "The Becnel Bunch," the video began with a takeoff on "The Brady Bunch," complete with our children singing their own version of the familiar TV theme song. The video continued with pictures and clips of each family member (including Chloe, our Labrador Retriever), family vacations, birthday parties, and other special events.

The highlight of the video, however, was a series of comments made by our children about each other and about our family. Here are some of their comments:

"He's definitely the person to hang around if you're in a bad mood. He will make you smile over the stupidest things. He has a love for people and a joy for life that I admire."

"She looks up to me and makes me feel important."

"Paige is my best friend. She's a blast to be around and has the true heart of a servant – a clean servant."

"I'm proud to have Moe as my Dad. He stands behind us no matter how crazy our ideas are. He brings our family together."

"Our family is now one. It's a big, exciting, funny family."

"We are one. We have grown together through the years."

At the end of the tape, our children had edited in this:

"Thanks for laughs

Thanks for the tears

Thanks for the last

Eight years.

We love you!"

After eight long years, our children were declaring – and finally *feeling* – that the seven of us were a real family. The video showed us that it was very important to our children that we had become a family unit. This realization was important enough to them to invest eight weeks collecting photos, preparing scripts and songs, and locating the equipment they needed to make a video honoring and celebrating our blended family.

On that anniversary, we commemorated not only eight years of matrimony, but how far we had all come since July 1, 1989, when our marriage united not only the two of us, but Paige's two daughters and Moe's two daughters and son. On that day, we began experiencing the struggles of making two separate households a single, united family.

To our disappointment, becoming a family did not happen quickly. Instead, the seven of us lived with the arguments, frustrations, disappointments, and day-to-day turmoil experienced by most blended families. Our new life included issues of children versus stepchildren, new rules and whose rules, competition for time and affection, new schools, and losing old friends and making new friends – again.

In the beginning, there were isolated moments of closeness, but no sustained unity or harmony. And there were many, many days when we wondered if we would ever become a real family, or if we would continue to function as a fragmented unit for the rest of our lives together.

But much to our joy, it did happen. After years of work and prayer, our fractured family was at last made whole. Our children finally came to enjoy being part of our family, and every member of our family finally came to appreciate and enjoy the others.

We are not saying that our family suddenly became, or has since become, perfect. And though it did require our time, work, and perseverance, we can take no credit for the transformation that took place within us.

Instead, we recognize our united family as a true miracle.

God has done awesome things in our family. We are amazed at the restoration from divorce He has created in our lives and in our children's lives. God promises His blessings to those who serve Him and seek His face. Our family is proof of those blessings.

We wrote this book to bring hope to other blended families who are struggling, and who truly want their new spouse and all of their children to become a solid, loving family unit. We encourage you to take comfort, knowing there is a Light that, when invited in, will pierce any and every darkness. That Light is Jesus, the Light of the World and the Light of Life.

As the Bible reminds us, "...the same Lord is Lord of all and richly blesses all who call on Him, for everyone who calls on the name of the Lord will be saved" (Romans 10: 12-13).

The same Lord who united our family is waiting to help yours. What He has done for the Becnels, He will do for you!

Moe and Paige Becnel

Restoration After Divorce

Blended families are made up of parents and children who have experienced either the death of a spouse or divorce. Before we begin, we must address the issue of divorce and God's forgiveness.

God's Word, the Holy Bible, is quite clear that divorce is to be avoided if at all possible. The Bible states, "I (God) hate divorce." (Malachi 2:16)

In most cases divorce is sin and there are great negative consequences to divorce. Divorce is usually the result of other sins, such as selfishness, mental abuse, verbal abuse (including criticism and sarcasm), lack of commitment and other sins that tear down relationships. There are some cases in which the innocent marriage partner has not sinned by divorcing, as in the cases of physical abuse, adultery, child abuse and child molestation by the other spouse.

In either case, divorce is painful for all involved. As people who have experienced divorce, we can certainly understand why God hates divorce. Divorce rips people apart and causes deep hurts that take a long time (and God) to heal. Divorce dramatically changes people's lives – including those of the extended family members – and altars plans not only for the short term, but for many years into the future.

Some people and church denominations believe that all past divorce is sin, and continues to be a sin in one's present life – that people are permanently "stained" by divorce, and that God will

6

not bless second marriages or blended families. This line of thinking implies that divorced people are not as good as those who have never experienced divorce, and that divorced people are not worthy of nor entitled to the abundant life Jesus came to give us.

As a result of this condemnation by society, some divorced people walk with low levels of hope, and low expectations for their future and the future of their children. We know of some remarried men and women who still carry a sense of failure because they have experienced divorce, and are hesitant to "admit" that they are now part of a blended family. They do not believe or have faith that the full life Jesus offers is for them

We believe there are two reasons why some people and churches have difficulty in easily and completely forgiving others. These reasons are linked.

First, people do not love others as God, our Father, does. The level of mercy and grace that a person extends to others is directly proportional to the level of love that person has for others.

Secondly, because of this lack of love, a spirit of competition is prevalent in the world. Jealousy and envy are rampant in America. Some people do not want others to succeed, or to rise above their circumstances. They prefer others to walk defeated.

We do not believe that God wants His children to live unforgiven and defeated. Instead, we know that God is a God of restoration. When there is true repentance from our sins, God brings forth complete restoration in our lives.

The Scripture has much to say concerning the forgiveness of all sin, including those leading to divorce. The following Bible verses come to mind.

"If we confess our sins, He is faithful and just and will forgive us our sins and purify us from all unrighteousness." (1 John 1:9)

"He forgives all my sins and heals all my diseases; He redeems my life from the pit and crowns me with love and compassion." (Psalm 103:4)

"...as far as the east is from the west, so far has He removed our transgressions from us." (Psalm 103:12)

"...it (love) keeps no record of wrongs." (1 Corinthians 13:5)

"The thief comes only to steal and kill and destroy; I (Jesus) have come that they may have life, and have it to the full." (John 10:10)

If there is true repentance (turning away from your sin), God forgives completely. The slate is clean. There is no stain. You are as "white as snow." (Psalm 51:7; Isaiah 1:18)

God wants to restore you. He loves and cherishes you and your new family.

Chapter 1

God's Plan for Blended Families

By Paige Becnel

I can only begin by saying that Moe is a wonderful husband and we have a great family!

Our wedding day was fun and full of children – five between the two of us. All of the girls were dressed so beautifully, and Jordan was quite handsome. Rose petals and daisies, ribbons and white lace, the perfect music, family and friends, and the loving bride and groom. It was perfect.

After the ceremony, Moe and I flew to Los Angeles for our honeymoon, enjoying seven blissful days alone together. We arrived back home late on a Friday night. I'll never forget the joy of opening the door to find four of our five children asleep on the floor beneath a huge, hand-lettered sign reading, "Welcome home Mom and Dad!"

But all too soon, the honeymoon was quite literally over.

Real life set in, and along with it, conflict.

I did not like the way Moe corrected my children and he did not like the way I corrected his. My daughters came to me with pitiful faces full of hurt, telling me what "he" said they could or could not do. The rules I had established in my former home were suddenly challenged by the rules Moe had established, and vice-versa.

"You don't discipline your children enough!"

"Why don't your children listen when I correct them?"

"My children are not allowed to do that!"

"Well, my children are!"

I thought he was wrong. He thought I was wrong. It was a never-ending cycle. Moe and I began to resent each other. Each set of children began to resent their new parent.

What had happened to our perfect family?

Struggles of Blended Families

I prayed fervently every day for our new family. Even through the hard times when Moe and I did not see eye to eye, I always spent time with God, interceding for every member of our family. God, I thought, would surely honor those prayers.

And He did. But not the way I *thought* He would.

During the early years of our marriage, I wondered if our house would ever feel like a warm, loving home. I felt a dark cloud hanging over Moe and me. Just when I thought we were making progress in an area of our marriage or in relationships within our family, something would break loose and hit us blindside.

Moe and I never seemed to agree on anything when a decision had to be made concerning the children. The same statement was present in every conversation. "If you would do this, then I would do that." We never really solved anything, only walked away confused and hurt by each other.

I became more and more frustrated, and remember saying more than once, "Why even try to talk about it? We never solve anything anyway."

I sometimes felt I prayed in circles. I would search the scriptures for answers, and find reassurance. God would sustain me in His joy and praise. But then I would find myself facing the same wall I thought I had already climbed. Was God even listening to me in my prayer time? Did He see us flailing about, trying to make something of all this?

During this time, I happened to see a television documentary on blended families. The program featured interviews with members of blended families and discussed the struggles they were facing. But then, something was said that really caught my attention. A psychologist stated that it takes a blended family an average of four to eight years to "gel," and finally feel like a real family.

I literally stopped what I was doing. I remember thinking to myself, "that may be true for some families, but we live and breathe for God. Doesn't the scripture say that nothing is impossible with God?" (Luke 1:37) The rest of the world may have had to wait four to eight years, but I did not think that would be necessary for the Becnels.

"God," I prayed, "did You hear that? Four to eight years to gel? You are bigger than that. With You on our side, we will become a true family in less time than that!"

Looking back, I'm glad I didn't know what was ahead. Because even the Becnels, a family who lived and breathed for God, took seven years to mesh, melt together, and become one family.

But even though it took longer than I had hoped, God was always and still is in control. He heard my prayers loud and clear – a lot clearer than I ever thought He did.

God's Knowledge of Blended Families

God knows us much better than we give Him credit for. After all, He created us, and created us for a purpose.

"Before I formed you in the womb I knew you." (Jeremiah 1:5)

"'For I know the plans I have for you,' declares the Lord, 'plans to prosper you and not harm you, plans to give you a hope and a future.'" (Jeremiah 29:11)

One day in prayer, I questioned God as to His knowledge of a blended family. Can you imagine questioning God's knowledge? It sounds so disrespectful, but God has a way of extending His grace abundantly to our lives over and over again.

I sat quietly, listening for that still, small voice that comes from deep within your soul and ministers to your heart. Then I heard, "My Son was a stepchild, and part of a blended family."

That statement startled me. I reread the story in Matthew chapter 1 of Jesus's conception, Joseph and Mary's quiet marriage, and Jesus's birth. How many times I had read this passage, yet never seen that Joseph was Jesus's stepfather. What an awesome task God had given to Joseph, a simple carpenter – to raise the Son of God. The very breath of God was in their family!

God Has a Plan

But God did not stop there. Instead, He went on to reveal to me a most precious lesson about my family through the creation story.

"In the beginning God created the heavens and the earth. Now the earth was formless and empty, darkness was over the surface of the deep, and the Spirit of God was hovering over the waters." (Genesis 1: 1-2)

This was exactly how I was feeling and seeing my family – empty, formless, and definitely dark. God nailed that one!

I was also intrigued by the use of the word "hovering" in this verse. "Helicopters hover," I thought. Before they land on a designated spot, they hover close, looking and preparing, then finally land to perform the mission they were sent to do.

In Greek, the word "hover" means "to brood over." Webster's defines "brood" as "to cherish, to love, or to hold dear." Now this was stirring my spirit! How, I thought, could

God cherish a dark, formless, empty, nothing? And then the still, small voice answered, saying, "I saw potential in nothing."

What a powerful revelation! God sees potential in darkness, in emptiness, and in nothingness. Why? It is a place in which His grace and power can create something beautiful.

The darkness and emptiness in our family was not a threat to God. Instead, it was a chance, an opportunity for Him to breathe upon us and work a miracle! He was hovering over our family, looking for the perfect spot to begin His mission. And He found it, right in the middle of our hearts.

The creation story goes on to say,

"And God said, 'Let there be light,' and there was light. God saw that the light was good, and He separated the light from the darkness." (Genesis 1: 3-4)

God's first act of creation was to create light, and to separate the light from the darkness.

In our case, God had to separate the light from the darkness in our lives. There were many dark, void spots in our family, which I believe are present in most blended families. What are those dark areas?

- No bonding between you and your spouse's children.

- You have less patience with your spouse's children than with your own.

- You are sterner and less tolerant with your spouse's children than with your own.

• You do not love your spouse's children as you do your own.

• Your new children do not respect your authority.

If you see these dark areas in your own life, don't worry. God has a plan. And He will reveal it to you in His time.

God's Timing

When I heard the psychologist say that it usually took a blended family four to eight years to gel, I was sure that God would work on our family much faster than that. After all, He was God! He had everything under His control.

Eight years later, I asked God why it had taken so long for us to become one. He took me back again to the creation story. I realized then that God could have created the earth in one day. One moment. *One second.*

Instead, He invested six days, completing everything according to His plan, in His timing.

Why? The answer lies in Genesis 1: 3-19. God spent four days separating the light from the dark, the sky from the expanse below, the seas from the land masses, the evening from the morning. He created fleshly life on the fifth day, Adam on the sixth, and rested on the seventh. God spent four days separating and getting things in order for His ultimate creation– us.

Before he could unite our family, God had a lot of separating to do in Moe and me. He had to separate our thoughts from His will for us, our pride from His humility, and our past from what He was trying to do for us now.

Our Thoughts

Our thoughts can so often get in the way of what God is trying to do for us. We question God with endless whys and why nots.

Remove your thoughts of doubt about what God can do in your life. Make way for Him to give you the prosperous future He desires for you.

"'For I know the plans I have for you,' declares the Lord, 'plans to prosper you and not to harm you, plans to give you a hope and a future.'" (Jeremiah 29: 11)

Be patient as God's plan for you reveals itself. So often, God gives us His plan for our lives, then we doubt His magnificent power because things don't move quickly enough to suit us. Truth is, God would probably work a lot faster, but we get in His way.

Have you ever tried cleaning your house with your whole family at home? It's almost impossible. You just finish vacuuming when someone spills crumbs all over the floor. You've just put the mop away when someone comes in the back door with mud on his shoes.

More than once, I've watched Moe try to mow the lawn, only to stop to move a bike, a water hose, a golf ball, or any one of a dozen items that someone in our family has added to the landscape.

Obstacles like these make your work more difficult and time consuming.

But what about God's work on you? Do you make it difficult for Him? Do you place your pride in the way of His work on humility? What about taking a left turn when His will is clearly to the right? Has His construction in the area of patience been slowed because you've been stomping your feet, rolling your eyes, and reminding God that you have a time schedule?

Our negative thoughts and flawed human reasoning are like muddy shoes, trampling all over the work God has done. Instead, we must be patient, and give God the time He needs to create a new thing in us. Step back from the work zone, and let God finish what He has begun.

Our Pride

The biggest area God had to work on for Moe and me was our pride. Our refusal to let go of certain things that seemed so important to us, including areas of parental discipline, made mountains of molehills.

God had to take time to teach us to sacrifice ourselves instead of taking from each other. We had to become less rigid and more flexible, warmer instead of colder, and give up *our* way for *His* way.

Pride only serves to hurt, separate and destroy. There is no truth in pride. Lay it aside and let God's humility take charge of your heart.

Our Past Baggage

God also had to remind us over and over again that our past was not a stumbling block for Him.

His future for His children is so much greater than we could ever imagine. His will for you is so powerful and awesome.

God spoke this to me one day: "The biggest dream you have for yourself is My smallest thought for you."

Only after He had finished separating and putting things in their proper order did God begin to create. Then He did a perfect job, creating so much with such precision and care. Then, the last day of creation was a day of rest.

You and your new family are a part of God's wonderful masterpiece. And once you make God's plan a part of your life, your day of rest is on its way.

"He will bestow on us a crown of beauty instead of ashes, the oil of gladness instead of mourning, and a garment of praise instead of despair." (Isaiah 61:3)

God loves blended families. Do not give up. You can and will make it. But you cannot accomplish this alone.

"'...Not by might nor by power, but by My Spirit,' says the Lord Almighty." (Zechariah 4: 6)

In Greek, the word for "spirit" is the same as the word for "breath." Allow God's Spirit to take charge of your heart and your home. Allow God to breathe on you.

Our Prayer for You

Father God, we pray for this blended family and all of their needs, which are being brought to You today. We know how close You are to them right now. You never leave them nor forsake them. Show Yourself to them and let them feel Your breath in their lives. Strengthen them in their journey to bring their family together as one to serve You. We love You and give You all praise. Amen.

Chapter 2

Two Must Become One

By Moe Becnel

If you were previously married, death or divorce has destroyed the family unit you and your children had. In either case, all family members have suffered deep hurts.

But there is very good news for your new family. One of God's promises to His children is that He will restore us from any calamity.

"I will repay you for the years the locusts have eaten...." (Joel 2: 25)

After experiencing death of a spouse or divorce, people seek restoration of what has been lost – self esteem, companionship, finances, a family environment for their children, and wholeness for their future family.

God's restoration in your life and in your new family will always take place in accordance with principles found in the Bible. Before we go any further into the subject of blended families, we need to look at what God intended marriage to be like.

God's Principles for Marriage

Why are we discussing marriage relationships in a book on blended families? Blended families face very different and very difficult challenges. Your success in becoming a loving, blended family requires a very strong husband/wife relationship. The strength of your new family is based on the foundation of your marriage, and the strength of the foundation of your marriage is dependent upon the foundation of your relationship with God.

Your marriage must be based on God's principles for marriage, in which the husband and wife become one. Whether your marriage is your first, second, or third does not matter. God's principles are the same.

Let's take a look at the account of the creation of the first family, found in the Book of Genesis.

"Then the Lord God made a woman from the rib He had taken out of the man, and He brought her to the man. The man said, 'this is now bone of my bones and flesh of my flesh; she shall be called woman, for she was taken out of man.' For this reason a man will leave his father and mother and be united to his wife, and they will become one flesh." (Genesis 2:22-24)

This scripture outlines three key instructions for a successful marriage – leaving father and mother, uniting to your wife, and becoming one.

Leaving Father and Mother

God has a reason for telling couples getting married to leave their father and mother. The above scripture identifies what can be a monumental negative influence in a marriage – parents and extended family.

God is telling us that the new relationship – the marriage – must be stronger than the relationship with your extended family and friends. Your relationship with your spouse must be more important than, and must supersede, all other relationships in your life.

Paige and I know of several marriages which have failed due to parental interference. We have seen marriages in which one of the spouses has never truly left his or her father and mother. Effectively, this spouse has one hand on the marriage and one hand on the extended family. There is a lack of covenant relationship between the husband and wife.

Both spouses' relationships with their parents must change. Extended parents and family are to be loved, honored, and respected, and parental advice can be of great value, but the married couple is no longer under the extended parents' authority.

Two people cannot become one if other people – including extended family members or friends – are allowed to be involved in the decisions in their marriage. Extended parents should never interfere in or criticize their married children's decisions. *All final decisions belong to the marriage.*

If there is not a relationship change between each spouse and his or her parents, the marriage relationship will never become what God intended it to be.

The subject of extended families is discussed in further detail in Chapter 7.

United to His Wife

God instructs a man entering into a marriage covenant to attach to, cling to, cleave to, and hold onto his wife. I really like Webster's definitions of the word "unite:"

- to combine or conjoin, so as to form one

- to incorporate in one

- to join in interest, affection, or the like

- to ally

- to couple

- to cause to adhere

- to attach

- to become one

- to become incorporated

- to concur

If you were to attach yourself to a large tree, it would require both of your hands and arms. You could not attach or cling to a tree while partially holding onto the tree and partially holding onto something else. There would be no true union.

Likewise, spouses must make a two-handed covenant with each other. *Your spouse must take the highest place of honor, respect, and admiration in your life, excepting only to your relationship with God.*

God made a covenant relationship with us. It is comforting to know that God is attached to us and that He clings to us. The words "attach" and "cling" also describe God's intent for every marriage.

Two Shall Become One

Genesis 2: 24 is read during many weddings for good reason. The husband and wife are to become completely one in every way – in body, in mind, and in spirit.

We all understand the simplicity of becoming one in body, but many marriages and families falter because they never become one in mind and/or in spirit. In fact, the most unhappy marriages I have seen are those in which the husband and wife are not one in mind or spirit. They have different interests, different goals, different beliefs, different ideas, and different agendas. They do not agree on anything of significance. They do not enjoy doing the same things, or for that matter, enjoy being with each other.

Please realize that spouses must become one. The marriage vows alone do not make them one. The vows are the commitment that each will work to become one. Becoming one is not an event, but a process, just as a small seed becomes a mature tree.

When I was studying the ingredients for successful relationships, God spoke these words to me:

The strongest love relationship is based on mutual love, mutual honor, mutual respect, mutual admiration, mutual need, and mutual want.

These are powerful words, describing powerful acts of caring for another person. This type of relationship requires complete giving of yourself.

The Bride of Christ

"Husbands, love your wives, just as Christ loved the church and gave himself up for her." (Ephesians 5:25)

To understand that scripture, let's look at how God loves the church, the Body of Christ, which the Bible describes as the Bride of Christ. Take a moment to ponder these questions and answers:

Does God love you?

Yes! God demonstrated His love relationship toward you by giving His Son Jesus Christ as a sacrifice for your sins. God refers to Christians as the "Bride of Christ." Jesus died so that you could live, and have more abundant life.

"For God so loved the world that He gave His one and only Son, that whoever believes in Him shall not perish but have eternal life." (John 3:16)

Does God honor you?

Yes! God honored you by adopting you as His Child. He is the ultimate example of a loving father toward us – our provider, protector, healer, restorer, counselor, guide, and lover of our souls. We are heirs with Jesus to the Kingdom of God. (Galatians 3:26)

Does God respect you?

Yes! God respects us so much that He put His only plan for building His eternal Kingdom in our hands. God does not have a contingency plan if His church does not accomplish His plan for His kingdom. (Matthew 28:18)

Does God admire you?

Yes! God must admire you, for He created you in His image and His likeness. (Genesis 1:27) He also predestined you to be conformed into the image of His son (Romans 8:29) and created a customized plan for your life. (Jeremiah 29:11)

Does God need you?

Yes! God does not need your talents and abilities, but God needs you as a receptacle for His love. Love is not love until it is given away. Loving you brings God fullness. It is why He created you.

Does God want you?

Yes! God wants you as His child and His partner. God created man for fellowship and relationship with Him. He placed an emptiness in you that only He can fill, so that you would seek Him. Look at how Jesus, the Son of God, came to serve man; how He latched onto 12 men to teach, fellowship with, love, and serve them; how in the end, He called them His *friends*. (John 15:15)

Now, in Ephesians 5:25, God instructs us to apply the same relationship He has toward us, His church, to our marriage relationship.

A husband and wife are to have mutual love, mutual honor, mutual respect, mutual admiration, mutual need, and mutual want toward each other. A husband and wife should look for ways to bless and serve each other.

God has given you a spouse who is a jewel in your crown. Bless your spouse at your own expense! Consider your spouse, or *make* your spouse, your best friend.

Keep in mind that there is no love relationship at all when we are in a relationship merely to meet our own needs or desires. We have no love relationship with Wal-Mart or our local grocery. In the same way, we have no relationship with God if we only come to Him when we want or need something.

People who enter into a marriage for the purposes of improving finances, filling the void of loneliness, having someone to cook and clean for them, or meeting their other needs usually wind up with a strained relationship. Acceptance and love become performance-based, and the needy spouse becomes a burden to his or her mate.

By placing expectations on people to be a certain way or to do certain things, you only set yourself up for major disappointment. God must be your source, your provider, and your strength. Only then will you serve your spouse rather than expecting to be served.

As God meets your needs and desires, you then have a fulfilled life with which you can love and serve your spouse.

As you work to build your relationship with your spouse into a "best friend" relationship, consider the following thoughts.

- God made you and your spouse unique. God loves diversity! He deliberately made every person unique, with different personalities, looks, skin color, hair, voices, accents, heights, likes, and dislikes. It is God's *intent* that we all be different. Do not try to change your spouse's personality.

- Never compare your new spouse with your former spouse.

- Never compare your new spouse to your father or mother. Do not expect your spouse to parent, clean, cook, or act like your parents did.

- Make every effort to not offend your spouse (your best friend).

- Add excitement to your relationship. Do different things together. Try your spouse's hobbies. Avoid the "routineness" that can develop in relationships.

Our Prayer For You

God, we do not always understand the mystery of how only You can make two of us one in a marriage relationship. Help this husband and wife to serve each other, understand each other and love each other for who You created each to be. If change needs to take place, let each spouse be willing to let the change take place in themselves first. Thank You for loving this family. Amen.

Chapter 3

Divisions Within Families

By Moe Becnel

Many blended families do not function as a whole family unit, but exist with multiple divisions within.

Words and phrases like "his children," "her children," "my rules," "your rules," and "you discipline yours and I'll discipline mine" are common to blended families.

Satan has all types of families worldwide on the defense. Many families have been pushed back to the goal line, with Satan ready to score a victory over them. Too many marriages and families are struggling. They live with hurts, offenses, and bitterness, deal with rebellious children, and see no way out. Too often, parents stick their heads in the sand and assume all is well, or hope that the situation will somehow fix itself. Such thinking only ensures defeat.

The devil wants to kill, steal, and destroy your new family. He has some special tools that he uses exclusively on blended families. As a result, blended families face significantly more challenges than natural families in becoming a successful, solid, loving family unit.

Satan had the Becnel family on the defensive until, through prayer, God began exposing the devil's playbook. You see, the devil is not very creative. He has been using the same old plans to kill, steal, and destroy for thousands of years. The only new twist comes when he focuses his plans on you and your family.

God warns us of Satan's age-old plans in the Bible "...in order that Satan might not outwit us. For we are not unaware of his schemes." (2 Corinthians 2:11)

In this chapter, we will expose some of the weapons Satan used to come against our family, and how God helped us fight back, and gave us the victory.

God's Principles for Families

We must emphasize to husbands and wives the need to be on the offensive – fighting *against* Satan and fighting *for* your family. We get on the offensive by applying God's principles and developing the character of Jesus in each family member.

Let's begin by looking at some of God's principles for families. God created the first family when He created Adam and Eve in the Garden of Eden. According to the Bible, God visited with Adam and Eve regularly. God's hands were in the midst of their family.

It is God's desire to make your new family a *true* family, built on strong relationships and abounding in love. Only the love of God can make that happen. God wants to be in the midst of the re-creation of your family, and God's hand *must* be in it.

"Unless the Lord builds the house, its builders labor in vain." (Psalm 127: 1)

We cannot successfully build a loving family and home without God's help. His principles are necessary to achieve His design for a family.

Divisions Within Families

Matthew 12:25 describes a problem facing many families today.

"Jesus knew their thoughts and said to them, 'every kingdom divided against itself will be ruined, and every city or household divided against itself will not stand.'" (Matthew 12:25)

These are powerful words from Jesus! Satan's main strategy is to look for a place of dividing. If he is allowed to find it, the erosion of the family begins.

Erosion is a slow but deadly process. Years and years of everyday storms cause the crumbling of big things – the Grand Canyon, entire mountain ranges, pyramids, your family, and even your life.

If a husband and wife allow divisions to remain between them or within their home, the marriage and family will eventually fail. At times, all families, natural or blended, allow divisions to become established. Because they are established subtly, we may even be unaware of divisions within the home. But the hairline cracks created by arguments, insults, offenses, disrespect, and pride, among other things, can grow into bigger and bigger divisions. Realize this – *all divisions are the work of Satan for the purpose of destroying the family unit.*

Typical areas of division in blended families include:

- His children   vs.   Her children
- His beliefs   vs.   Her beliefs
- His rules   vs.   Her rules
- His discipline   vs.   Her discipline
- His extended family   vs.   Her extended family
- His wants   vs.   Her wants
- His goals   vs.   Her goals
- His pride   vs.   Her pride

And remember, *perception is reality.* Divisions may exist, even if you do not think they do. If your spouse sees them, they are there. If your children see them, they are there. And they will remain until you and your spouse make changes.

Signs of Division

Following are some symptoms of division in blended families. Take a quick test to see if there is any "unblendedness" in your home.

- "You discipline yours and I'll discipline mine" are common statements.

- You only speak pridefully of your natural children.

- You talk only of your children, while your spouse talks only of his or her children.

- You have high grace toward your children, but low grace toward your spouse's children.

32

- Two sets of rules exist in the home.

- Two sets of expectations exist in the home.

- You and your spouse cannot come to agreement on one set of rules and discipline.

- New children call the new parent by their first name, or by "Mr. or Mrs. Name."

- Your one-on-one time with children is spent only with your natural children.

- The term "step" is used in the home (stepfather, stepmother, stepsister, stepbrother).

- You feel as though you are raising someone else's children.

- Your grown children are not a vital part of your new marriage.

- Your spouse has grown children, and you do not consider them a part of your life.

- "They have other parents" is your excuse for not treating your spouse's children as your own.

- You do not love your spouse's children as your own, nor do you think you can.

- You think, "My spouse's children do not want me in their lives."

- You do not consider your spouse's grandchildren as your grandchildren.

Even if many of these symptoms exist in your home, do not lose heart. Many of them existed in our home, as well. The good news is that you have identified the devil's work of dividing. Now you can take action, get on the offensive, and start making your home what God intended it to be.

We will now look at some of the divisions that existed in the Becnel family, and tell you how God directed us to handle certain situations.

Respect for the New Parent

It is natural for parents to want to protect their children, if they have been hurt by death or divorce. There is a strong tendency for parents to nurture and protect their natural children in a new family, even to the point of going against the new spouse.

Children in a new blended family may not like the new family environment or the new parent. The children may see the new parent as an outsider who is not only taking their parent's time away from them, but is now disciplining them as well. They may manipulate, challenge, and bring division between you and your spouse in order to get what they want.

Manipulation occurs in all homes to some extent, but in the blended family environment the child often challenges or "attacks" the new parent. This is probably the hardest area of all to overcome, and requires a great deal of courage on the part of both parents. Spouses must stand up for each other in front of and sometimes against the children – even when you think your spouse is wrong. *Respect of the new parent is a must. The natural parent must demand that his or her children respect the new parent.*

Advice:

- Stand up for your spouse and demand that your children respect their new parent. Failure to do this will cause the new spouse to resent both the new children and you.

- Discuss disagreements between you and your spouse away from the children.

- Do not "spoil" children because they are children of divorce. I agree that your children are hurting from the previous broken home, and possibly from rejection by the other natural parent. But lack of discipline and letting them get away with misbehavior only makes matters worse.

- Until they have had time to adjust, handle children with great grace.

"Step" Syndrome

The primary objective of a blended family is to establish a loving, caring relationship among everyone involved. Unfortunately, the widely-used terms "stepmother" and "stepfather" automatically put the new parent in a different category than the natural parent. The same applies to the terms "stepsister" and "stepbrother."

Several years ago our son came home from church crying. When we asked what was wrong, he said his new sister had introduced him to some of her friends as "my stepbrother." Use of these terms puts all new relationships within the home into a lower category. They indicate, "I live with you, but we really do not belong together."

We all have a need to belong and to be loved. Why use words that divide?

The Becnel family decided to not use the term "step" in our home. We gave all of our children the option of calling us Mom, Dad, Moe, or Paige. All of our children wanted to call us Mom and Dad, and have done so since.

As a new parent builds a loving relationship with new children, the new children may want to call the new parent Mom or Dad. More than simple names, these are terms of deep affection and belonging.

But what if the child's natural parent (your former spouse, or your spouse's former spouse) objects to his or her child calling someone else "Mom" or "Dad?" What if you are hurt by the idea of your natural child calling another person "Mom" or "Dad"?

I can address this question from personal experience. When my children began calling my former wife's new husband "Dad," I was hurt and upset. I felt they were stealing my right to parent. But eventually, I realized this was a hurt I had to let go, if for no other reason than the happiness and well-being of my children.

Remember, you cannot control what goes on in someone else's home. Consider the use of an affectionate term for your child's new parent a blessing – a sign that your child is happy and comfortable in his or her other home. And even if your child chooses to call his or her new parent "Mom" or "Dad," you will always be the natural parent. And with the exception of yourself, no one places more importance on that relationship than your child.

Advice

• Give the children the option of calling the new parent by his or her first name, or "Mom" or "Dad."

• If your children choose not to call the new parent Mom or Dad, use first names, leaving off the "Mr." or "Mrs." These terms are too formal, and are not conducive to building close relationships.

Your Children / My Children

We know of many blended families in which the husband and wife continue to function as single parents. The theory, "You take care of and discipline your children, and I'll take care of and discipline mine," is common in blended families.

In most new blended homes, an initial effort is made to blend the role of parenting between the natural and new parents. The blending process can be very frustrating, however, and frequently causes the parents to retreat from that effort. It just seems easier for you to take care of yours, and your spouse to take care of his or hers. But is it right? No! It is a division in the family, and if it is not removed, it will build resentment and disrespect between the new parent and the child, as well as between the husband and wife.

If you and your spouse are not working together to function as a family unit, the children will not try either. They are looking to you for guidance. You and your spouse must bond together first. The children will respect your efforts and follow suit.

Advice:

- The new parent should set goals to build relationships with the new children. This takes time. Remember, love is a choice. You must first choose to love your entire new family.

- Take time alone with each new child and get to know them, their personalities, and their likes and dislikes. Just showing interest in them goes a long way. One-on-one activities and attendance of school functions and extracurricular activities with the new children will build the relationship. The more quality time you spend with them, the more you will start to love them, and the more love and respect they will have toward you.

- Remember, *you* have to make the time, not everyone else. Change starts with you.

- Natural parents should allow the new parent to participate in the parenting process, but, at least in the early stages, the natural parent should carry out the discipline. This concept is further discussed below.

Discipline

A husband and wife may enter into a blended family with the assumption that they now have parental authority over all the children in the family. Not so – at least not right away!

Discipline by a new parent who does not yet have a loving relationship with the new children usually causes hurt feelings and resentment. God gave me a revelation in this area. *Love must cover discipline.* Discipline cannot cover love.

"Because the Lord disciplines those he loves, and he punishes everyone he accepts as a son." (Hebrews 12: 6)

This scripture tells us that God disciplines and punishes *those He loves and accepts as sons and daughters.* Unless, or until, we truly love our new children and accept them as our sons or daughters, we have no right to discipline them.

"Wait a minute!" you say. "If they are going to live under *my* roof, I have a right to discipline them." I understand how you feel, but hear me out. When you were a child or teenager, if someone other than your parents tried to discipline you, what did you do, and how did you feel? You probably thought something like, "What gives him the right to tell me what to do?" or "You are not my parent!"

Yet, you accepted discipline from your Mom or Dad. Why? Because they loved you, and you knew they loved you. Your new children feel the same way about discipline from their new parent. This will eventually change as they feel the new parent's love toward them grow.

When discipline covers love, the implication is, "When you do what I say, *then* I will love you and respect you." This is no different than discipline in the Army or from a police officer. This type of "conditional love" is not really love at all, but is more closely related to tolerance. When discipline or punishment is dispensed from someone who does not love the recipient, respect fades and resentment builds. *Love must cover discipline.*

Advice:

- Sit down with your spouse and come to agreement over reasonable rules and resulting discipline that will apply to the whole family. Then stick to them. Don't make excuses for your children when they break the rules. Be consistent with everyone.

- When your new child misbehaves, express the need for discipline to your spouse, but let the natural parent administer the punishment until your love for that child increases enough that you have earned respect, and the right to discipline. Do not be in a hurry for this to happen. It is a slow but steady process. Give the relationship the time it needs to grow.

Submission After Independence

Adults who have been thrown back into the world of being single through death or divorce have had to become independent and self-sufficient for themselves and their children. This in itself is good.

When these people remarry, however, they are often faced with a spouse who has conflicting likes, dislikes, habits, and rules for the new home. It is not easy to give up your way of doing things when you have been functioning independently for a long time.

Advice:

• All successful relationships require giving. Give so that new, *agreed-upon* rules, not just *your* rules, can be established.

Things do not have to be done your way. You are no longer on your own. Give yourself, and your ways, to your spouse and new family.

Double Standard

A double standard exists within a home when parents treat individual family members differently. This is usually a symptom of different levels of love (i.e., you love your natural children more than your spouse's children). Again, different rules, different levels of mercy and grace, and inconsistency in discipline generate resentment. Children in your home must all be treated the same by you, regardless of whether they are your natural or new children.

Advice:

• Agree that the need to treat everyone in the family equally is of great importance. Then take time, a sheet of paper and a pen, and work out an agreeable set of new rules that you and your spouse can live by. Agree that any required discipline will be administered fairly. When grace is extended, it must be extended to everyone.

• Always treat others the way you want God to treat you – with great levels of compassion, mercy, grace, and forgiveness. This applies to your natural and new children as well.

Child Wants Natural Parents Back Together

Children of divorce miss their other natural parent, and may long to see their natural parents reconcile. This is a big struggle for many children. Children need time and opportunity to understand and accept the new family situation. Be honest with your children, explaining the situation with loving kindness. They may not like what they hear, but the truth will set them free.

Advice:

• Extend grace and be gentle – your child is hurting! Participation in the new home, helping a child to feel he or she is a part of the new family, can help bring healing.

• Make your child aware of the benefits of the new family – every cloud has a silver lining.

Child Wants To Live With Other Natural Parent

Parents may find themselves faced with a child who wants to leave the domicile home to go live with the other natural parent.

There may be legitimate reasons for such a desire.

Perhaps the child simply misses the other parent. Should this child then move to the other parent's home, he or she would probably begin to miss the parent he or she was previously living with. This is normal. We strongly encourage both natural parents to work through this with the child. The goal is not for one parent to "win" over the other, but to come up with an arrangement that everyone agrees upon.

However, the child may want to live with the other natural parent because the child does not feel wanted or accepted, or does not feel that he or she is a part of the domicile home. Perhaps the child does not get along with the new parent, or does not like the new family's set of rules. Such situations call for tender loving care. Realize that most people, including children, will not want to leave a place where they feel loved. In fact, people usually migrate to the place where they are loved the most.

Either of the scenarios above causes a heartache for the domicile parent, who does not want to lose the child. Should this situation arise with your new children, be sensitive toward your spouse. Imagine how you would feel if your child wanted to leave.

If you are the new parent and there is tension between you and your new child, you must take action. You are the adult. It is your responsibility to love the child and make the child feel vital to the family.

Love your spouse's children. They are an integral part of your spouse's life. If you do not love his or her children, you do not truly love your spouse.   Your spouse and his or her children were one before you entered the picture. You cannot separate them.

Failure to love the children will divide the home even further. Resentment will build between you and your spouse. *If that child goes to live with the other natural parent because of tension or rejection from you, your spouse will resent you.* You will have caused the separation of a relationship between your spouse and his or her child, a relationship that was vital to them.

Advice:

- If the child does not feel a part of the new family, the real issue must be uncovered and dealt with.

- If the new parent does not love the child, the new parent must take responsibility and develop a relationship with the child. The new parent/new child relationship is equally as important as the husband/wife relationship.

Your Spouse's Need for Security

Another division that Paige and I struggled against was insecurity. Both spouses must feel secure in the marriage relationship, and certain things I did – albeit unintentionally– threatened Paige's security.

The greatest of these involved conversations between myself and my former wife concerning our children. I was certainly not trying to make Paige feel insecure, but it happened anyway. When I explained to Paige that I had no interest in my former spouse, her comment was always, "but she is the mother of your children."

If your relationship with your former spouse is threatening to your new spouse, it is your responsibility to do whatever is necessary to make your husband or wife secure.

A second area which tested Paige's security involved our house. After the wedding, Paige and I resided in the house that my former wife and I had built. Paige struggled to make this house her home. At first I thought the feelings Paige had about the house would simply go away. But this was not the servant attitude God wanted me to have toward my wife. Instead, we agreed to make a few simple changes – new room colors, wallpaper, curtains, bedspreads – that reflected Paige's personality and taste.

Other actions that contributed to Paige's insecurity included my frequent fishing and hunting trips and my failure to take up for Paige when my extended family was rude to her.

By this point, you may be thinking that Paige was being possessive and controlling. This was not the case. Instead, I had to learn that women are sensitive, and that husbands must respect the intricacies of how God made women. My actions were not bad in themselves, but through these actions, I made Paige feel that other people and activities were more important to me than she was.

How did we address these insecurities? Common sense.

Advice:

- You are both responsible for providing security in your new home. There is no place in your new marriage and blended family for an overly friendly relationship with your former spouse if it causes your husband or wife to feel insecure. When I had to speak to my former spouse regarding our children, I did so with Paige present, and conducted the conversation in a business-like manner. If I spoke to my former spouse from the office or when Paige was not with me, I made sure I told Paige about the conversation, demonstrating that I was not hiding anything from her. Finally, I considered Paige's input in decisions regarding my children, who are now a part of her life.

- I understand the realities of paying alimony and/or child support. Your new spouse will, too. But beyond that, your devotion and resources must be toward your new spouse. Any additional resources that you direct to your former spouse must be given with your spouse's agreement.

- Your home should be a reflection of your new life together. Make sure both spouse's personalities and tastes are reflected in your home.

- No relationship, job, sport, or activity should be more important than your relationship with your spouse.

As you give, you will receive, and receiving always carries a multiplication principal. The more you invest in your marriage relationship and your new family, the greater you will receive not only from that relationship, but from God. *Love, dignity, honor, respect, want, and high esteem are earned only through investment in relationships.* These are the treasures that your spouse and family will give back to you.

In our case, I had to learn not only to give, but to give in, and to give up certain things. Did I quit hunting and fishing altogether? No. I did not have to. Once I demonstrated to Paige that she was more important to me than these activities, they no longer made her feel insecure. I continued hunting and fishing in moderation – sometimes accompanied by Paige and our children. But most importantly, I realized there are much more important things in life.

- We mentioned earlier that extended family can have a negative impact on blended families. This is such a critical subject that we have devoted another chapter to the extended families (see Chapter 7, "Interference From Extended Family").

Our Prayer For You

Father, we ask You to touch this new family as they take the time to nourish each other and grow together. Help them establish grace as the foundation of that growth, and gentleness as the foundation of discipline. As they work together, bring light on their darkness and new life into their new world. We thank You for giving us Your mercy every day, and Your love as a foundation for us to work from. Amen.

Chapter 4

Ingredients For Healthy Blended Families

By Moe Becnel

Chapter 3 identified and discussed divisions that can cause significant problems in a marriage and blended family. We will now consider certain positive aspects of relationship building which are a part of all successful marriages and blended families.

The following are key ingredients to building healthy, solid, loving relationships.

Individual Wholeness

Individual wholeness is being secure as an individual, knowing who you are to God and knowing who God is, or wants to be, to you – your Father, provider, protector, deliverer, and healer.

God called Himself, "I am." (Exodus 3:14) This means God is whatever you need Him to be, because He is your most excellent Creator and Father. No person on earth, not even a husband or wife, can fill that role in your life.

If you are not whole, you have nothing to give to a spouse, to your children, or to your new children. Instead, you wind up being a taker in the relationship. Rather than trusting God to be your provider, you are dependent on another person, probably your spouse, for your needs and your happiness.

God created us not only with a body and a mind, but with a spirit that allows us to fellowship with Him. This part of man is vital. Consider the different religions of the world, all seeking to serve the spirit man.

Consider, too, the many places people search in an effort to fill the emptiness within. When we try to fill our emptiness through relationships with men and women, we always come up empty and disappointed. Wholeness in each of us comes only when the spiritual part of our lives is fulfilled, and only God can fill it.

You may have experienced hurts in your past through broken relationships, either from death or divorce. God needs time to heal your hurts, preferably before you move into another marital relationship. If you are remarried but still carry hurt, anger, bitterness, low self-esteem or resentment toward others from your past, those negative feelings will affect everyone around you.

Now is the time to be set free. Build your relationship with your Heavenly Father through a relationship with Jesus Christ. Look to God as your source, and set yourself, as well as your spouse and family members, free.

God As The Center of The Family

There is so much truth to the statement, "the family that prays together stays together." If God is truly made the center of the home, the home will prosper.

"Blessed is the man who does not walk in the counsel of the wicked or stand in the way of sinners or sit in the seat of mockers. But his delight is in the law of the Lord, and on his law he meditates day and night. He is like a tree planted by streams of water, which yields its fruit in season and whose leaf does not wither. Whatever he does prospers." (Psalm 1: 1-3)

Now replace the word "man" in this scripture with the word "family." The message? The family who delights in the law of the Lord prospers.

As a husband and wife pursue a daily, loving relationship with God, allowing God to take control of their lives, they will prosper, and as a direct result, their family will also prosper.

All families must establish a high standard of righteousness and excellence in their homes. Parents are responsible for setting goals to achieve righteousness in their home and identifying obstacles that hinder the accomplishment of those goals.

If you are not already attending church as a family, start now. Find a church where you and your children will be challenged to follow the principles of God. Read and study the Bible as a family.

An Orderly Home

The Almighty God and creator of the universe is a God of order.

All of God's creation is put together intricately and perfectly. Consider the human body. Every organ, gland, and appendage has a specific purpose, and is positioned to serve that purpose. The level of detail God gave Noah in order to build the ark and the instruction God gave Solomon for the building of the Temple – even down to the type of material and color for each item –

reflect God's attention to detail and order.

Likewise, a *family* must have order, and *will* have order if God is made the center of the home.

Disorder prevents the home from functioning as a place of love, nurturing, and security. A disorderly home lacks peace and joy. Husbands and wives have a responsibility to pursue order in the home.

What is (and is not) reflective of order within a family?

- Order is a family with loving, considerate parents.

- Order is a family with obedient children.

- Order is a family with reasonable schedules.

- Order is a family with goals, and strategies for accomplishing those goals.

- Order is a family who lives by high moral standards.

- Order is a family with a neat, clean, organized residence. External appearance often depicts what is inside a person; the same can hold true for a family.

- Order of leadership for a family is God first, husband second, and wife as co-leader.

- Order is *not* a family with mindless regimentation, enforced with strictness.

- Order is *not* a family with rules but without discipline. Rules have no purpose if they are not enforced.

Giving

The relationships that last are giving relationships.

God gave! We are His children because God gave His Son, Jesus Christ, to redeem us. And we, in turn, are to give. Unfortunately, we live in a selfish society. Television, newspaper, and magazine advertisements are designed to increase our wants and to feed our natural desires. Most marriage and family problems can be traced to selfish acts. Creating a loving family requires just the opposite response. Husbands and wives, your family blessings will come according to the level of your giving. Throughout the Bible, God teaches the principles of giving and receiving, and sowing and reaping.

"Give, and it will be given you." (Luke 6:38)

As we give, we receive. It never works the opposite way. As you (parents and children) give into the lives of your new family, you will receive blessings from God. The receiving process may not, and likely will not, happen quickly. But do not stop giving. God's Word is faithful and true!

One day Paige and I were struggling over an issue, and neither of us wanted to give in to the other's wants. I felt I had already given enough, and that it was Paige's turn to give.

Then God spoke these words to me: *Until you are on your knees and have washed her feet, you have more to give, and you will only receive in accordance with your level of giving.*

Ouch! God had exposed my flesh and my pride. After all, Jesus did not hesitate to wash His disciples' feet. It was an act of loving. The water was insignificant – Jesus was washing His disciples with His incredible love.

Love requires action, and that action requires giving. This includes giving in – acknowledging that things do not always have to be done your way.

Here are a few simple ways you can give of yourself to your new family.

- Determine your spouse's desires, ambitions, and dreams. Be in accord with those and help your spouse accomplish them.

- Find out your children's likes, dislikes, hobbies, friends, and teachers' names. Be plugged into their everyday life!

- Introduce your new family to your coworkers.

- Display your family to others.

- Have fun together. Do things everyone in the family likes to do, not just what you want to do.

Silence

Emotions run high on occasion in any relationship, and people tend to say things they later regret. When your emotions run high, do not react hastily. Calm down before an issue is discussed any further. As the saying goes, "Never miss an opportunity to shut up."

"My dear brothers, take note of this: everyone should be quick to listen, slow to speak and slow to get angry, for man's anger does not bring about the righteous life that God desires." (James 1: 19-20)

I cannot count how many times I prejudged situations with Paige and with our children, even before I had heard all of the facts. I jumped to conclusions and reacted before I should have, creating hurt feelings, lack of respect, and embarrassment. I learned the hard way that it can be good – very good – to just shut up.

High Grace

God has been so gracious toward you and me. Even before we knew God, He gave to us His Son, who came to serve us and die for our sins that we might live an abundant life. God forgives us every day – as often as we ask Him to. In turn, we must forgive and extend grace to others.

In Matthew 18: 23-30, Jesus told the parable of the unmerciful servant. The servant owed a large debt to the king. The king forgave the servant of his debt. Yet, after being forgiven, the servant went to a man who owed him a much smaller debt and demanded payment. When he could not pay, the servant had the man put in prison.

How often we act like the unmerciful servant! We have been forgiven so generously and so many times, yet we discipline our children over the smallest, usually insignificant things.

One day a friend and I were talking about rules we had established in our homes. During the course of the conversation, I realized that I demanded a lot from my children, and many of my demands were over minor issues. I felt the tug of God to examine myself, and how I had established relatively insignificant rules in our family. God changed my heart. I became more gracious toward my family.

Sometimes our biggest expectations of other people are over the smallest things. We must learn instead to set other people free. This is grace!

Walk in grace. Treat people, including your spouse and children, as you want God to treat you when you are not faithful. Don't miss any opportunity God has for you to show grace to your family – your entire family. Remember, true grace does not exclude anyone.

Our Prayer for You

Father, we ask You to teach this new family to walk in Your incredible grace. Give them the courage to wash every member of their new family with love, extending much mercy and grace toward every person. Pierce their hearts with a fresh love and respect for both spouses and for every child. We thank You for always being there when they need You most. We love and thank You.

Amen.

Chapter 5

The Children's Perspective

By Moe Becnel

Children in a blended family almost always come from a past of pain, either from death or divorce. They have suffered deep hurts and deep loss they did not deserve.

Children of divorce have seen the security of their natural family fall apart. Quite often, the children are shocked by the divorce – the parents pretended all was fine until the "announcement" came that one of the parents was leaving.

Children often feel responsible for the divorce, and ask themselves "What can I do to fix our family?" This is followed by feelings of helplessness that come with the realization there is nothing they can do to mend the family unit. Their lives may become chaotic, marked by feelings (real or imagined) of rejection by one or both parents. Anger rises up, and children may begin exhibiting many dysfunctional behaviors in response to their conflicted emotions. These behaviors may include poor grades in school, disrespect toward their parents or other adults, lack of trust in other people, and involvement with the "wrong crowd."

Every child has a different story – no two situations are alike. Yet all children who have experienced divorce have these things in common:

- They do not have much to celebrate.

- They must have hope.

- They must have healing.

Everyone needs hope and healing in his or her life. Even King David, a man after God's own heart, needed hope and healing. David declared,

"I am still confident of this: I will see the goodness of the Lord in the land of the living." (Psalm 37:13)

Like their parents, children of divorce need restoration in their lives. God has a prosperous plan for your children. God wants to use you and your new family as an instrument of His hope and healing in their lives.

I recall a day early in our marriage when Paige and I gathered our family and sat on our living room floor in a circle. Paige and I apologized to each child for the fact that he or she had been put through a divorce. Divorce was not what we wanted, and was certainly not what we wanted for them. We then told them that we wanted our new family to be a real family, and we wanted to be their Mom and Dad in this home. We also apologized for all the times we had treated any child unfairly, held a grudge against them, or failed to make them feel a part of the family.

After the apologies, we allowed each child to share what was on his or her heart. We cried together, then prayed for each child. What a breakthrough we had! Our time of sharing made a difference in everyone's attitude, and created a kinder, softer respect and appreciation for each other. It was a time of healing for us and a definite turning point for our family!

Children entering a blended home are forced to deal with several new issues, including instability, acceptance, new rules, new personalities, new environment, competition between new siblings, and new authority.

As previously divorced or widowed parents, we must be considerate of our children's feelings and struggles. Remember, they did not ask for this lifestyle.

Following are but a few of the complex issues children in blended families must face.

The Need for a Strong, Consistent Family Environment

Children whose world has been shaken need to find stability again. They usually miss their other natural parent and their old, familiar surroundings and lifestyle. Their other natural parent may be deceased, or may ignore or reject them.

The new home may also feel unstable – the children may fear the new family will fall apart as the last one did. As the teenage son of one of our friends told her, "Every time a man leaves you, he leaves me, too."

Above all, children of divorce need a solid family foundation. Children learn and develop character based upon their environment. Your children will mimic you. As they grow up, they will most likely say what you said and do what you did, and will even parent as you have parented them. The new home should exemplify a strong family environment, and serve as a positive role model for the children's own future families.

It is the responsibility of the husband and wife to produce a positive atmosphere of stability, built on love, caring, and grace from both parents. *If the only love the child feels in the new home is from his or her natural parent, the home atmosphere is divisive.* The child will not feel a part of the new family, and will not find a source of healing from his or her past hurts.

If you do not love your new spouse's children, you will bring division into your home. You cannot truly love your spouse without loving his or her children. Your spouse and his or her children are one. If you think of them as non-connected, separate people, you will likely treat them differently. Any conscious or unconscious actions to separate the natural parent and his or her children will only result in separation between you and your spouse.

Dealing with Varied Disciplines

When divorced parents remarry, their children usually find themselves faced with one set of rules, or lack thereof, at the domicile home, and another set of rules, or lack thereof, in their other natural parent's home.

You will surely hear statements like, "My dad lets me do that at his house," or "My mom lets me talk on the phone any time, and as late as I want." It is best if the two natural parents can minimize the differences in rules, but that is seldom likely.

The solution to this issue is not to relax or eliminate rules, for all children need discipline. Instead, explain the reasons for the rules you have established in your home. If the rules pertain to moral issues, show your children God's reasons for the rules you have established.

Understand that you cannot control the other home or your child while he or she is there. Be patient with your children if they question or challenge the purpose of certain rules they must obey in your home, but not in the other home. Have sound reason, and be consistent.

Someone Is Always Missing

Children of divorce lead fragmented lives.

In an article in Newsweek magazine entitled, "My Long-Distance Life," teenage author Nick Sheff describes his life as a child of divorce. Nick's divorced parents lived 500 miles apart; Nick spent most of his childhood commuting back and forth to see them. Whether it was his mom, his dad, or his friends, Nick grew up missing someone all of the time.

"At the age of five, I discovered what all children of divorce know: you're always missing somebody," Nick writes. "After all those back-and-forth flights, I've learned not to get too emotionally attached....Before I have children of my own, I'll use my experiences to help make good decisions about whom I choose to marry. However, if I do get a divorce, I will put my children's needs first. I will stay near them no matter what happens."

Children of divorce lead complicated lives, logistically and emotionally. As Nick Sheff so eloquently points out, someone is always missing. The experience is even worse for teenagers.

While their friends from school – who are very important to them – are planning parties and get-togethers for the weekend or the summer, children of divorce are leaving town to spend time with their other parent. These children continually miss out on school activities and activities with their friends.

While there is a strong need for children to spend time with both parents, they do not deserve this stressful lifestyle. Parents, what are you subjecting your children to? Do you consider their feelings and how your decisions affect them?

As a caring parent, please do your best to make life easier on your children.

The Other Natural Parent

Children will always love their other natural parent – never expect them not to. If you have experienced divorce, you may still harbor some ill feelings toward your former spouse. As many times as I forgive, ill feelings always seem to creep in. However, I know I cannot expect any of our children to disrespect or not love their other natural parent, no matter what I feel toward that parent. That parent is and always will be their parent, and will always have some influence on them.

Realize that your former spouse is loved by God, and that God requires us to forgive, to respect, and to do good toward him or her. We avoid using the terms "ex-spouse" or "ex." These terms connote that the person is marked, a has-been who is no longer of value. God does not see your former spouse that way. God always sees value, potential, and hope in everyone.

Advice:

- Never ask about the other parent's life or lifestyle, unless there is sound reason to believe that there may be a negative situation or abuse that affects the child. Keep questions personal to the child only, such as, "What did you do this weekend? Did you have fun?" then move on to other subjects.

- Do not discuss issues concerning the other parent in front of the children, unless it is of utmost importance to have the children's input. If your children make remarks about their other natural parent's behavior, lifestyle, or choice of discipline, do not comment. It is very important that you do not make any remark, other than a positive one, about the other natural parent.

- Keep in mind that while you may not like the other natural parent, he or she is still a vital part of your children's lives. More than likely, your children have already seen you exchange harsh words with your former spouse. If tension exists, keep conversations between you and your former spouse few and non-emotional. Avoid confrontations. If confrontations do take place, spare your children from having to hear them.

- Admittedly, former spouses can be very difficult. Some former spouses continue to try to gain or maintain control over a family that is no longer their own. If this is you and your former spouse has remarried, please let your former spouse get on with his or her life. Your former spouse does not need you to tell him or her how to run things. Give he or she some space, and your former spouse will likely give you some respect.

Special Events

Like all children, children in blended families celebrate birthdays, graduations, holidays, weddings, and dozens of other special occasions.

It is important to your children to have both their natural parents and their new parents present for these occasions. However, many children of divorce do not experience such parental support because the natural parents do not get along and refuse to be in the same place with the former spouse.

The children wind up having two separate birthday parties, or having only one parent there to see the home run, the commencement ceremony, or even the wedding. At best, both natural parents attend major functions, but demonstrate such ill will and cause such friction that the *child* is made miserable.

Two of our daughters got married within two years. Both weddings were marked by tension between former spouses and former in-laws. Frustrated and disgusted, one of our daughters asked me why her natural parents could not "get along like adults" for her wedding. It was a very good question, to which I did not have a good answer.

As we mentioned earlier, children of divorce did not ask for their situation. Children need their natural parents to be amicable, and to act like adults. Tension between former spouses must be eliminated for the welfare of your children.

Children should grow up in an atmosphere of love, mercy, and grace. It is the responsibility of all parents – new and natural – to create that atmosphere. Your children are worth it.

Your former spouse may have caused great pain in your life. But if you are not walking in forgiveness, you are only hurting yourself and your children. Holding a grudge will choke the life out of you, your natural children, and your new family. You do not have to be best friends with your former spouse to act in kindness and to be polite and gracious toward him or her.

Advice:

• Put yourself in your child's place. Imagine what it would be like to have the people you love the most continually at odds with each other. Then make a commitment to change the ill relationship between you and your former spouse.

• Do not speak in harsh tones.

• Don't be on the defensive.

• Change your attitude by looking for the good in your former spouse – remember, there is good in everyone.

• Pursue true, complete forgiveness of your former spouse. Keep in mind that merely *tolerating* your former spouse is not the same as *forgiving* him or her. Instead, think about how much God has forgiven you. Then ask God to help you forgive your former spouse, and pray for a blessing over him or her.

• Communicate with your former spouse for the benefit of your children. When appropriate, attempt to have face-to-face meetings with your former spouses and the new spouses to discuss your children's events, education, or other special needs. Always begin such meetings in prayer, asking that an attitude of cooperation and peace prevail. *Never attempt such a meeting without prayer.*

The Pawn

Often a child of divorce is placed between his or her natural parents for the convenience of the parents. The child becomes the communicator (often of harsh messages), the messenger, and the go-between.

Your children do not want to be in the middle of two non-communicating, uncooperative adults. They should not be expected to act as your go-between. Your children did not ask for any of this. Quit using them as your pawn.

To parents who use your children to bring division into your former spouse's new family – *watch what you sow.*

Your children are watching, and more than likely know that *you* are the troublemaker who is stirring up the water at the other home. They feel your resentment and prying, and do not appreciate it. In your efforts to make life difficult for your former spouse, you are hurting your own children.

Advice:

• Stop pumping your children for information about your former spouse's life.

- Stop making it difficult for your former spouse to spend time with his or her children.

- Stop using your children to deliver letters, messages, or checks to your former spouse. Children are not to be our messengers or couriers. That is the parents' responsibility. Using children for such activities only puts them between you and your former spouse, and that's a tough place for anyone to be.

- If you are guilty of any of the above, resolve to end this negative behavior *now*. Start by asking for your children's forgiveness. Then ask God your Father for His forgiveness. Then forgive yourself.

- Focus on rebuilding your own life. We are so proud of people we know who are going back to school, learning new trades, serving in areas of the church, or extending a helpful hand to those in need. They are moving on and into the new things God has for their lives, and so can you.

Our Prayer For You

Father, we ask You to help the parents in this blended family respect the feelings of their children. Show them the hearts of their children and what they are feeling, and help the parents be more understanding. Forgive these parents for the times they may have put their children between the natural parents. Help the parents walk in forgiveness toward the former spouse. Thank You for showing them Your loving hand in parenting. Amen.

Chapter 6

Responsibilities of a Stepparent

By Paige Becnel

Becoming a good new parent (stepparent) is one of the toughest assignments in the world. Loving and parenting a child who was not born to you is not a natural thing.

But when you marry a man or woman with children, you also marry his or her children. Parent and child are intricately attached; you cannot separate them.

Jesus called children to Himself, touching each one of them. Why? Because He wanted to serve them, love them and bless them, just as He did and still does the rest of God's creation.

"People were also bringing babies to Jesus to have Him touch them. When the disciples saw this, they rebuked them. But Jesus called the children to Him and said, 'Let the little children come to Me, and do not hinder them, for the kingdom of God belongs to such as these. I tell you the truth, anyone who will not receive the kingdom of God like a little child will never enter it.'" (Luke 18:15-17)

We are here to serve our children, to bless them, to love them, to nurture them, and to help them in every way possible. We are to lead them along the right paths in life.

This role may seem more, well, *"natural"* for the natural parent, but new parents are also charged with this responsibility. How can new parents do this? Following are two ways to begin.

Be Yourself

In the movie "Stepmom," Julia Roberts plays the stepmother-to-be to two children of divorce. In the beginning, Roberts' character exhausts her energies trying to become what and who the children's natural mother wants her to be. But only after she decides to stop imitating someone else and be herself do her new children begin to respect and love her.

Your new children want and need the *real* you, not some figment of your imagination. Show them who you really are. Don't try to impress them with wild antics, dress styles, or attitudes. Don't try to prove that you are "hip," or that you've "got it together."

Instead, simply show them that you are willing to make this family union work for them, their mother or father, and you. Laugh with them, cry with them, and talk to them about things going on in their lives.

They may not open up to you right away, but given time, love, patience, and the real you, they *will* come around. I can attest to that myself.

Develop a "Spirit of Adoption"

It may not be possible for you to legally adopt your spouse's children. In most cases, the other natural parent would not allow it.

What I am suggesting instead is that you *mentally* and *emotionally* adopt. Consciously make your new children a vital part of your world.

The word "adopt" comes from the Latin adoptare, which literally means "to choose." Webster's defines "adopt" as "to take by choice into a relationship." You made a choice to marry your spouse, along with his or her children. Now you must choose to blend together as a family. The children, no matter what their ages, are a vital part of your union.

The Bible describes such a "spirit of adoption," through which you and I are made sons and daughters of God.

"Because you are sons, God sent the Spirit of His Son into our hearts, the Spirit who calls out, 'Abba, Father." So you are no longer a slave, but a son; and since you are a son, God has made you also an heir." (Galatians 4:6)

"I will be a father to you, and you will be My sons and daughters, says the Lord Almighty." (2 Corinthians 6 :18)

If you do not have this spirit of adoption toward your new children, ask God to help you find it. Just the conscious act of asking will unify your family in an incredible way.

"But you are a chosen people, a royal priesthood, a holy nation, a people belonging to God, that you may declare the praises of Him who called you out of darkness into His wonderful light." (1 Peter 2: 9)

God chose us to be His own special people. He chose *you*. You are royal, holy and belong to God. He has called you into His light.

Those precious little ones who are now living with you are waiting for *you* to call them into *your* light, *your* world, *your* love. Make a choice to choose them.

Advice

- Remember, what's good for your natural child is good for your new child, too.

- Make all of the rules the same for everyone.

- Give every child a chance to express his or her thoughts at family meetings.

- Don't pick favorites.

- Don't treat any child as a "Cinderella."

- Arrange schedules so that everyone goes on vacation together as one family.

- Spend equal amounts of money on each child at Christmas and on birthdays.

It took our family a while to understand the concept and realize the benefits of the spirit of adoption discussed above. But as we grew into loving and treating all of our children equally, our family became a place of comfort, joy and peace. Appreciation for and acceptance of each other reached new levels.

On our last three anniversaries, Moe not only brought me a card and a gift, but also brought our children cards and presents. The occasion has become not just Paige and Moe's wedding anniversary, but an anniversary of our blended family – an anniversary of our new children's lives with us.

Call your new children your sons and daughters. Make them your heirs. You can fill the void in their hearts left by divorce. You can be the tool God uses to heal their broken hearts.

God is doing the very same thing for you.

Our Prayer for New Parents

God, we pray for the new parents in this blended family. Help them to continually walk in grace toward their new family. Remind them daily that You created them to be exactly who they are and to be as no one else. Give them the strength to make the right choices each and every day. Thank You for choosing us and loving us as sons and daughters. Amen

Responsibilities of a New Father

Moe asked me to write this section, not because I am a father, but because I could see what my children needed in a new father.

If you already have natural children, you may be thinking, "I'm already a father. What's the difference between parenting my natural children and my new ones?" For answers, let's look at Jesus's family life with Mary and Joseph.

Most of us know the story of the Immaculate Conception. Joseph and Mary were engaged to be married when Mary became pregnant with God's Son through the Holy Spirit. God sent an angel to Mary to reveal to her the details of His plan, and to explain the remarkable circumstances surrounding her pregnancy.

Now imagine Joseph's reaction upon hearing this news. His fiancée was pregnant, and the baby was not his. And no matter how much he cared for and respected Mary, could Joseph *really* believe her explanation for the pregnancy?

While we will never know all of Joseph's thoughts, one thing is certain. Joseph truly did love Mary – enough to save her life. Jewish law dictated that a woman found pregnant out of wedlock be stoned to death. Instead, Joseph made plans to send Mary away quietly to have her child.

But then, an angel visited Joseph and confirmed to him that this child was of the Holy Spirit. And wonder of wonders, God had chosen him – a simple carpenter – to care for and parent the Son of God! He was to marry Mary and give her a good home in which to raise their son. *Their* son – now that was a thought. How could the Son of *God* be *their* son? Because Joseph was to be Mary's husband. When he married Mary, he married her unborn child.

Can you imagine being called to become the stepfather of the Son of God? What a challenge Joseph faced! How did he handle it? He provided the same love, discipline, and care for this child that he would have and later did provide for his own natural children.

You may be thinking, "But this was *God's* Son!" So is the child you are now a stepparent to. Is not God the creator of all things and all people? Do you believe that you are a child of God? So are any new children who have become part of your new family. They need the same love, discipline, and care that you would give to your very own child.

You may be thinking, "They already have a father." So did Jesus. But this did not excuse Joseph from his responsibilities. It is not an excuse for you, either. In fact, scripture provides us with clear insight into Joseph, Mary, and Jesus's blended family.

"Now Jesus Himself was about thirty years old when He began His ministry. He was the son, so it was thought, of Joseph." (Luke 3:23)

Those around Mary and Joseph *did not even know* that Jesus was not Joseph's natural son.

I can imagine this family – Mary, Joseph, Jesus, and Mary and Joseph's other children (Mark 3:32) making their way through the town of Nazareth. I can see Mary and Joseph talking with neighbors while their children played together, maybe engaging in a game of chase or hide and seek among the merchants and their wares. I can picture Mary and Joseph keeping a careful eye on each child, including Jesus. I can imagine Mary and Joseph correcting them, carrying them, running after them, laughing with them. No wonder people never suspected that Jesus was not Joseph's natural son.

Luke Chapter 2 provides another look at Joseph's relationship with Jesus. Every year, Joseph took his family to Jerusalem for the Feast of the Passover. One year, a full day into their journey back home, Mary and Joseph noticed that twelve-year-old Jesus was not with them.

The Bible does not say that *Mary* went alone to look for *her son*. Instead, scripture tells us that both *Mary and Joseph* went back to look for Jesus *together*. They were both frightened, I am sure, and looked diligently for their son for three days before eventually finding Him in the temple courts. (Luke 2:41-47)

This account tells us that Mary and Joseph's was not a "he is your son" arrangement. This was their family, and Joseph held himself responsible for the well-being of his son.

Joseph loved Jesus as his son, his firstborn son, his and Mary's son. This does not mean that Joseph did not honor God as Jesus's Father, but that while Jesus was in his care, Joseph would treat Him as his own.

Just as Joseph was responsible for Jesus, you are responsible for the well-being of each member of your new family. You are not taking the place of your new children's birth father (although some of you may actually be acting in that role), but you have just as much influence over them. You may or may not see your new children every day, but what you say, how you discipline, how you behave, and your relationship with them is vital. The idea of "mine" and "yours" should not affect the way you care for and protect your new family. You are responsible for them.

Some children may have a hard time accepting a new father. Understand that they did not choose you; you chose their mother and she chose you. The children may feel as though you have taken their mother's attention away from them; in a way, you have. But if you give them enough understanding, love, and patience, you will find that time will heal them of this hurt.

One of my daughters had a very hard time with my marriage to Moe. It wasn't that she did not like him, he just took my time away from her. The best way to handle such a situation is for you and your spouse to spend time with each child, one on one. This time leads to the creation of special moments between each child and each parent. Everyone feels special, needed, and wanted.

In our case, I took my daughter to lunch, to the movies, or to get a snowball – just the two of us. But I spent time with our other children as well. When we did things together as a family, my daughter was expected to participate. Finally, she began to understand that we were all one family now, and that while I did not love anyone more than I loved her, I also did not love anyone less. Moe continued to love and be patient with her through this difficult time, and it paid off. Rest assured, love will break through any barrier.

"It (love) always protects, always trusts, always hopes, always perseveres. Love never fails." (1 Corinthians 13: 7-8)

In another example of his close relationship with Jesus, the Bible tells us that Joseph taught his stepson the same family business he taught his natural sons – carpentry. (Mark 6:3). Together, they learned to make something out of nothing, and to repair those things which were broken.

God our Father is also in the carpentry business. He makes wonderful things out of our nothingness, and fixes what is broken in our lives. A blended family can be a wonderful restoration of what was broken.

In tough times, we tend to question God and His understanding of where we are. God sent His Son to an earthly father whom He had personally hand-picked. In the same way, God has personally hand-picked *you* to father children who are not your own, yet have become yours through your marriage to their mother.

Will you take the challenge that Joseph took? Will you be there when your new children need you, and even when they think they don't? Will you teach them the family business of restoration?

We pray that you will.

Our Prayer for the New Father

Father, God, we pray that each member of this family feels how important and special they are. We thank You that You hand-picked each member to be a vital part of this family unit. Teach this new father the same grace, patience, and love for others that was so evident in the life of Joseph. Fix what is broken in their lives, and build something in the areas of their nothingness. We love You and thank You for all that You do in us. Amen.

The Role of a Stepmother

Mention the word "stepmother" and the first thought that comes to mind is "wicked." The fairy tale stepmothers battled by Cinderella and Snow White seem to have become the standard image people have of a stepmother.

In the movie "Stepmom," the Julia Roberts character struggles against this image. But no matter how hard she tries, nothing she does is ever good enough, especially when her efforts are compared to those of the children's natural mother. Every encounter with her new children leaves her feeling like a failure – a flop who will never measure up.

As a new stepmother, I often felt the same way, struggling to define my role as a new mother. Then I realized a simple truth.

The role of a *new* mother is the same as the role of *any* mother.

Make a list of what you do or would do as a mother. You would love, nurture, train, teach, discipline, care for, encourage, and nurse. You would join carpools, make school lunches, chaperone field trips, teach to drive, shop for prom dresses, and baby-sit grandchildren.

You would partake in every aspect of your children's lives. And as much as possible, you should partake in your new children's lives.

Let's look at what scripture tells us to do.

"Train a child in the way he should go, and when he is old he will not turn from it." (Proverbs 22: 6)

This scripture is a standard for *all* parents, natural and new. Your job is to teach and guide your children in the right direction and path they should take. How do you do that? With lots of love, understanding, and patience. If the children you are parenting are new children, the same attitude of love, understanding, and patience is required. Otherwise, you will become the wicked stepmother.

Ask yourself, "how would I handle this situation if this were my *natural* child?" When Moe and I were first married, I had a difficult time being a good mother to both my natural children and my new children. After all, they already had a mother. I was not interested in taking on her role, too. Eventually, I realized that I was not replacing *her*, but that I had been given the chance to nurture and help raise a part of Moe.

I believe that God made the wife and mother the very backbone of a home. When my children are not feeling well, I am the one they want. When Moe comes home from the office, I am the one he wants to talk to. If something cannot be found around the house, they usually come calling for me.

On any given day, I hear:

"Mom, have you seen my school shirt?"

"Mom, did you put fruit in my lunch?"

"Mom, did you wash my shorts, yet?"

"Mom, can you pick me up from work today?"

"Mom, Mom, Mom, Mom!"

I hear these questions from *all* of our children (and from Moe, too). And I would gladly wash for, drive for, pack a lunch for, iron a shirt for, or do virtually *anything* for all of my children, new or natural.

We stated earlier that you might have more patience for your own children than you do for your spouse's children. I was often guilty of imposing stricter rules on my new children than I would have on my own. I overcame this by asking myself if the law I was laying down was the same rule I would ask my natural children to follow. The same goes for discipline. Would you discipline your own children the same way you are about to discipline your spouse's children?

Your role as a new mother is no different than your role as a natural mother. You are to train the children you have been blessed to help raise with the same love, care, and devotion you would your own natural child.

"Sons are a heritage from the Lord, children a reward from Him." (Psalm 127: 3)

All children are a blessing. God sees no blood, and neither should you. Remember, Jesus called the little children to Himself, and rebuked the disciples for trying to send them away.

"People were also bringing babies to Jesus to have Him touch them. When the disciples saw this, they rebuked them. But Jesus called the children to Him, and said, 'Let the little children come to me, and do not hinder them, for the kingdom of God belongs to such as these. I tell you the truth, anyone who will not receive the kingdom of God like a little child will never enter it." (Luke 18:15-17)

Are you calling the children in your house to you, or are you pushing them away? If you have been pushing them away, don't let guilt overcome you. Make a choice to right the wrong. Children are very forgiving, and so is God. Beginning today, surround yourself with *your* children.

Our Prayer for the New Mother

Father, we pray for this mother who longs to feel Your love for this new child she is raising. Give her an understanding of who she has been given the privilege to help raise. Help her to make sound decisions on behalf of the welfare of this little lamb. Give her the grace to go on when she feels overwhelmed, and the joy that only You can give when her days seem never to end. Extend Your patience when hers has been spent. Pour out Your blessing into her heart. We love You so much, we thank You for always staying by our side.
Amen.

Chapter 7

Interference From Extended Family

by Moe Becnel

"For this reason a man will leave his father and mother and be united to his wife, and they will become one flesh." (Genesis 2: 24)

This scripture identifies a potentially monumental negative influence in a marriage – parents and extended family. God is giving us a warning about extended families, and the negative effect they can have in marriage relationships. As we stated earlier, we personally know of marriages that failed due to parental interference. Add the special pressures unique to a blended family, and the situation becomes even more volatile.

Many blended families suffer from extended family members (parents, brothers, sisters, aunts, uncles, etc.) who refuse to accept a new spouse or new children. Such people either seem to have a limit as to how much love they have to give, or they seem unable to love across the bloodline.

We know situations in which extended family members do not like, and refuse to associate with, the new spouse and new children in the blended family. We have also seen situations in which extended family members give Christmas and birthday gifts to their grandchildren, nieces, and nephews, but ignore the new children in the same family. The new spouse and new children naturally feel hurt and rejected. Under this situation, the new family environment becomes a place of hurt and separation rather than a place of healing and wholeness.

Our friends Cedric and Laura, whose marriage created a blended family, shared this story with us. Cedric's extended family treated Laura's children differently than Cedric's natural children. Cedric's parents did refer to Laura's children as their "grandchildren," but still kept Laura and her children at arm's length.

When Cedric's father died, his mother decided to bestow a financial gift upon each of her grandchildren. She gave gifts to all of her natural grandchildren, but did not include Laura's children. Needless to say, this hurt Laura's children, hurt Laura, and hurt Cedric. Without words, a declaration had been made that Cedric's new children were not accepted as members of Cedric's extended family.

Cedric talked to his mother about the hurt feelings and, out of guilt, his mother later gave gifts to Laura's children. Knowing that she had given the gifts for the wrong reason, Cedric and Laura tried to give the money back, but his mother refused to take it.

Over the next several months, Cedric noticed that his mother and sisters were not friendly toward Laura and her children. Cedric finally asked his extended family why they were cold toward his new wife and children. Of course, they cited the money given to Laura's children. This time, Cedric and Laura did return the gifts.

Cedric and Laura did not really want the money anyway; they were already financially set. The money was insignificant compared to the real issue, which was *acceptance*. Cedric merely wanted his extended family to accept his new wife and new children. Instead, he learned the age-old truth that you cannot make people love one another.

Some of you may agree with Cedric's extended family. You may feel the stepchildren were not really a part of the extended family, and may sympathize with Cedric's mother for wanting to give gifts only to her "real" grandchildren.

If so, I ask you these questions:

- Would you feel differently if Cedric and Laura had adopted children together? If so, why?

- Why can't some people accept others into their family or into their world?

- What does God say about such a situation?

"If you love those who love you, what credit is that to you? Even sinners love those who love them. And if you do good to those who are good to you, what credit is that to you? Even sinners do that. And if you lend to those from whom you expect repayment, what credit is that to you? Even sinners lend to sinners, expecting to be repaid in full.

But love your enemies, do good to them, and lend to them without expecting to get anything back. Then your reward will be great, and you will be sons of the Most High, because he is kind to the ungrateful and wicked." (Luke 6: 32-35)

If we cannot love beyond the boundaries of our blood family, we are not walking in the love that God requires us to.

There is an old saying, "Blood is thicker than water." That may be true, but Cedric's wife and new children were not "water" to him. They were his new family, given to him by God, and he cherished them all.

Today I give you a new saying, based on Genesis 2:24.
Marriage and family must be thicker than blood.

When Cedric realized that his extended family did not accept his new family, he had three choices:

- Ally with his extended family

- Ally with his new family

- Do nothing, which is a negative decision in itself

The decision was not difficult to *make*, but was difficult to carry out. Basing his decision on Genesis 2:24, Cedric chose to stand by his new family and to stand up to his extended family. As long as Cedric's extended family refused to have a relationship with his new family, there would be no true relationship with Cedric.

If Cedric had decided to continue a side relationship with his extended family – going to see them without his wife and new children – he would not have been living as one with his wife. And if he had decided to do nothing, ignoring the situation and hoping it would go away, he would not have been standing up for his new family.

Why do we tell this story of Cedric and Laura? Because
many blended families have had similar experiences, often with
disastrous results. When a spouse abides by and makes decisions
based upon the actions, opinions, desires, or advice of his or her
parents and extended family rather than the opinions, desires, or
advice of his or her spouse, he or she is not living as God
intended.

"Honoring" versus "Obeying"

You may be thinking of another scripture, one of the Ten
Commandments, which seems to contradict this advice.

"Honor your father and your mother, so that you may live
long in the land the Lord your God is giving you."
(Exodus 20: 12)

Many grown children think honoring their parents means
they must continue to obey them. There is misunderstanding in
the meanings of the two words, "honor" and "obey."

Webster's defines "honor" as "esteem paid to worth, dignity,
exalted rank or place, reverence; any mark of respect or
estimation by words or actions."

"Obey" is defined as "to give an ear, to comply with the
commands of, to be under the government of, to be ruled by, to
submit to the direction or control of, to submit to commands or
authority."

The best professional baseball and football players are
"honored" when they are inducted into the Halls of Fame. This
does not mean we now need to obey them. We can honor

someone without letting him or her control our lives. Married children are to continue to honor extended parents and family. Yet, we are also to honor our spouses, and the *highest* place of honor must go to one's spouse.

Many parents resist the process of their children "leaving father and mother" when their children marry. They do not want to let go of the control they have had over their children for so many years. These extended parents sometimes revert to manipulation and guilt, making their married children feel guilty because they do not visit often enough, call every week, consult them with decisions, or otherwise do as they say. They may offer large financial gifts or loans in an effort to exert control over the couple. The controlling parents may also presume that their child's spouse is the cause for the inability to control their married child. This creates a poor relationship between the married child's spouse and the in-laws.

This is dysfunctional behavior. Extended parents must learn to let their grown children lead their own lives. No good parent wants their children to make the same mistakes they did, but parents should only offer advice to grown children, then let it go. The best service a parent of married children can do is to be there to help the children when and if they ask for help.

If you have controlling parents, you must stand up to them for the sake of your marriage. God's command to leave your father and mother and be united with your spouse means that your spouse now takes precedence over your parents and any other extended family.

Standing Up for Your New Family

The situation becomes even more complicated when new children are involved. We do not know why some people can love anyone and love easily, even to the extent of being foster parents or adopting children, yet others cannot accept people outside of their blood family. We will not attempt to address the causes, other than to say that, "hurting people hurt people."

We must emphasize, however, that such behavior by your extended families has great potential to cause problems in your new family. Spouses in a blended family must stand up for *every member* of their new family. You have the responsibility to guard your new family against hurt. If you do not guard your family, you then become another instrument of hurt to them. If you do not protect your new family from hurts by your extended family, you will be the cause of division and resentment in your home.

We know it is very difficult to stand up against your extended family. But when they are hurting people who have done nothing to them, to do and to say nothing to them is negligence on your part. Tough situations require tough actions.

Finally, keep in mind that while *you* cannot change people, *God can*. Pray over such situations. Ask God to change the hearts of the extended family members. Then be patient, and continue to protect the tender hearts of your new family.

Remember, God wants to bring healing and complete restoration. Walk in love toward everyone, even those trying to bring division in your life.

Our Prayer for You

Father, we ask You to pour out Your love into and around this new family. Give every family member favor with all extended family involved. Let there be a spirit of acceptance, the same spirit by which You accept us into Your Kingdom. Let no extended family attempt to divide this new marriage. We thank You that a strong love relationship is ever increasing in this family, such that nothing can cause separation or tear it apart. Amen.

Chapter 8

Vision and Purpose

By Moe Becnel

People need a purpose for their lives other than simply satisfying their own wants. Without future plans and goals, we live a very unfulfilled life. Many marriages and families have crumbled because neither spouse had any vision or purpose for the relationship.

The Bible describes this need for a vision.

"Where there is no revelation, the people cast off restraint." (Proverbs 29: 18)

When God created you, He also created a specific plan for you. Unfortunately, many people search for a lifetime for their purpose and never find it because they do not look to God for it. Even before you were born, God had a detailed plan for you and your new blended family laid out. He wants you to find it and walk in it. If you do not know God's vision or goal for your marriage or family, ask Him to show you.

Planning

It's been said many times that people and businesses do not plan to fail, they fail to plan.

Consider the many New Year's resolutions made every January – resolutions to draw closer to God, to lose weight, to be a better person, to get out of debt, and so on. Most of these resolutions are never accomplished. Why? Because no plans are put in place to achieve them.

The first step in successful planning is writing down your vision and purpose. When God gives you a vision, write it down.

"Write down the revelation and make it plain on tablets, so that a herald (or whoever reads it) may run with it." (Habakkuk 2:2)

At the beginning of each year, Paige and I had gotten into the habit of individually writing down goals and prayer requests – sort of a "wish list" of what we wanted God to do in our lives over the next year. For several years, the goals and requests remained individual and personal between God and each of us.

Then we decided to take the idea of goal-setting a step further by coming together in agreement over goals for our blended family. If Paige and I and our family were to become one, we needed to have a common vision and common goals.

We knew what we wanted our family to believe in and become, but we had never written it down. We decided to write a *mission statement* – an idea I brought home from work – for our family.

A mission statement is a written declaration, usually one or two sentences, describing the goals and objectives of an entity. Business executives write mission statements describing what the business must become or accomplish in order to be successful. Executives then use the mission statement to develop the company's plans, strategies, and annual goals. If such a process helps companies achieve success, we decided it could help our family achieve success, too.

So one night, our blended family sat around the kitchen table and developed a Becnel Family Mission Statement that focused on relational and spiritual issues. We allowed our children to participate in the process, asking what was important to them for our family to become and to accomplish. Allowing our children's input gave them a sense of ownership in the family goals.

Our final mission statement reads:

Becnel Family Mission Statement
The Mission of the Becnel family is
to serve Jesus Christ, our Lord, as a family,
to express God's love, God's respect, God's honor and God's
grace toward each other,
to respect and appreciate the individuality
that God gave each of us,
to share the love we have for each other
with those who need love, encouragement, and hope,
and to have fun!

The second step in the planning process is to establish a strategy for accomplishing your purpose or mission. Our mission statement strategy looks like this:

Strategy

Each family member will:

Pursue the character of Jesus in his/ her life

Establish a high moral standard

Stand up for righteousness, wherever he or she is

Abstain from "R" rated or questionable movies and television
   programs

Discipline with love and grace

Treat each person in our family as equals

Honor, respect and appreciate each other

Pray seven days for seven people

Be involved in our church

Be involved in outreach

Enjoy vacations and other fun activities as a family

You and your spouse obviously have goals, but have you
ever written them down? If so, have you then determined what
you need to do to accomplish your goals? If you set a high
standard of righteousness and excellence in your home with a
goal of achieving those standards, your children and family will
reap great dividends.

These key components should be a part of your family's mission statement:

- Jesus as the center of the home, with fruits of the Spirit in control

  "But the fruit of the spirit is love, joy, peace, patience, kindness, goodness, faithfulness, gentleness, and self-control." (Galatians 5:22)

- Pursuit of righteousness and holiness

- Love flowing within the family (spouse to spouse/parents to children/children to parents), as God the Father and Jesus love each other

- Love flowing externally (involvement with others outside your family), as Jesus loves us.

- What you want your children to learn

- Commitment to each other

- Unified dreams and desires

- Appreciation for each other

- Gratitude

Mission statements can be written for a variety of topics. A family will likely have multiple goals, including spiritual, financial, educational, recreational, and relational goals. A mission statement for each of these areas can help define purpose and direction, bring agreement, and create harmony and unity within the family.

The mission statement can also help identify solutions to problems that create conflict between the husband and wife, such as developing agreement on rules and discipline. In Chapter 3, we discussed potential divisions in a home. The process of sitting down and writing a mission statement will help identify these divisions and develop a plan to eliminate them.

Writing a Mission Statement opens the lines of communication between spouses. You may be surprised to find that the goals of your spouse are different than your own. Exploring the differences can help you meld the two, and work toward common goals.

Develop your own family mission statement, and see what writing goals and strategies down will do to bring agreement and focus to your family.

Our Prayer for You

Oh gracious Father, help this husband and wife to seek Your vision for their family. We know You have a supernatural purpose for them which will bring blessing to them first, and through them, to others. Help each family member to honor and appreciate each member of the family. Bless them today, and direct their steps into Your perfect will. Build their love for each other and their love for You. Be the Author and Finisher of their faith, as You promise to do. We love You and thank You for being intricately involved in their lives.
Amen.

Chapter 9

Prayer – An Awesome Thing

By Moe Becnel

We've saved the best for last – *prayer*.

The power of prayer has been the sustaining force that brought the victory – the breakthrough – in our lives and in our blended family. There were many days when Paige and I had no more emotional strength to continue trying to build our family. The struggles were frequent and intense. We were ready to give up many times. But the church in which Paige and I met had given us a strong foundation in the power of prayer. We had been taught about spiritual warfare, and through all the struggles of trying to build this new family, we knew the meaning of the next scripture.

"For our struggle is not against flesh and blood, but against the rulers, against the authorities, against the powers of this dark world and against the spiritual forces of evil in the heavenly realms." (Ephesians 6: 12)

We knew that our fight was not against each other, but against Satan and his army, who were trying to divide us and our family. But when emotions took over, we responded negatively against one another.

"What causes fights and quarrels among you? Don't they come from your desires that battle within you? You want something but don't get it. You kill and covet, but you cannot have what you want. You quarrel and fight. You do not have because you do not ask. When you ask, you do not receive, because you ask with wrong motives, that you may spend what you get on your pleasures." (James 4: 1-3)

We lack in every area of our lives because we do not ask for help in prayer, or because we ask for the wrong things with selfish motives.

The real solution to conflicts between spouses is to retreat from attacking and blaming each other, and to advance in prayer and in God's Word against the devil. Christians so often underestimate the power of prayer. *Prayer has been the overwhelming power that has produced the positive change in our hearts first, and then in our blended family.*

I intentionally repeat myself – God cherishes your new family! He wants to give you everything you need to build a successful blended family. But we only hear from God and gain His instruction when we spend time in prayer, in communication with Him, seeking His will for us.

Prayer Initiates Positive Change

Insanity has been described as "doing the same thing over and over and expecting different results." The same is true of our prayer life.

If we pray the same amount of time, with the same lack of zeal, with the same weak sacrifice and the same level of distraction, we cannot and will not experience change. If you need radical change in your life, your marriage, your new family, or your children, you need to radically change your approach to prayer.

All people resist change. It is very difficult to break habits. Multi-million-dollar businesses thrive on this fact – the "stop smoking" and weight-loss industries are just two examples. Because it is so difficult to change, we would rather change those around us, including our spouse and children, than change ourselves. We usually pray for God to change our circumstances, rather than praying for God to change us.

Unfortunately, in order to solve our problems, God most often needs to change *us*. The change almost always calls for more of the character of Jesus to become manifest in our lives – more love, more compassion, more servant-hood, more mercy, more grace, more holiness, more humility, less pride, less want, and less self.

You can initiate change in your life, and you do not have to do it alone. Your loving Father, the Almighty Creator of the universe and the detailed planner of your life, wants to help you. Just ask with a sincere heart, and be willing to change your heart. Realize the value of prayer.

For people to initiate a change in their life, they must want the change. And they will only want the change when they see enough value in making it.

In Luke 11: 2-4, Jesus taught His disciples how to pray; He gave them the Our Father. In Jesus's next statement to His disciples (Luke 11: 5-13), He tells them why they should pray, and tells them of the value of prayer. Jesus knew human nature.

He knew that the disciples had to understand the benefit and the power that comes from prayer before they would make prayer a permanent part of their lives. Just as showing them value got the disciples praying, it will do the same for you.

Hold Your Family Up in Prayer

Prayer also brings positive results in children. A person is never too young to learn to communicate and fellowship with their Heavenly Father. There is no reason why your children cannot pray with you or for you. They will learn to pray by hearing you and others pray. They will learn to pray by praying.

We exposed our own children to prayer at an early age. We attended prayer meetings to which we brought our children and expected them to pray with us and for us, though we did not expect them to pray for long periods of time. As a result, I have seen our family knit together more through prayer with each other than in anything else we could ever have done.

Our children will also testify to the power of prayer. In 1999, Paige and I took all of our children and one of our sons-in-law on a seven-day cruise in the Caribbean. Our oldest married daughter, who was four months pregnant, had a terrible bout of seasickness. Our 14-year-old daughter suggested we pray for her. Our family knelt beside her, encircled and laid hands on her, and prayed. It wasn't too long before she was feeling well enough to enjoy the rest of the trip.

Mom and Dad, you must set the example. When your children see how important prayer is to you, it becomes important to them. When they are included as a vital part of those prayers, they respect its power.

Husbands and wives should continually hold each other and their children up in prayer. Pray for all areas of your children's lives, including for healing from the pain of divorce or death of a parent, for Godly friends, for success in school, for purity, for spiritual growth, for fruit of the Spirit of God (Galatians 5:22), for Godly future spouses, for future ministry, and for taking authority over the spirits of rebellion, disobedience, strife, and manipulation. Pray against peer pressure, and for helping the child feel a part of the new family.

Set goals concerning prayer for your family. Consider these:

- Prepare your prayer each day – do not pray the same prayers day after day.

- Join a prayer meeting or attend prayer at church with your family.

- Set your alarm clock. Get up early to spend time with God.

- Pray specific prayers over each child.

- Ask you children what they want to pray for, and encourage them to pray.

Our Prayer for You

We close with a prayer that the words of the worship song below become your heart for your new family.

Breathe On Me

Breathe on me breath of God
Love and life that makes me free
Breathe on me breath of God
Fan the flame within me
Teach my heart and heal my soul
Speak the mind that in Christ we know
Take me to Your sanctuary
Breathe on me

Speak to me Voice of God
Soft and still inside my heart
Speak to me Word of God
Comfort, heal, restore with love
Teach my heart and heal my soul
Speak the mind that in Christ we know
Take me to Your sanctuary
Breathe on me

Epilogue

We have shared our heart, our struggles, our failures and our successes with you. We tell you now that blending a family isn't easy, and it doesn't happen quickly.

It requires sacrifice. Ouch! We all hate that word.

It requires patience – another tough one.

It requires considering all those around you, even children, as more important than yourself.

It requires extending grace – treating others as God treats you.

It requires setting goals and guidelines for yourself and your family.

It requires an adoptive spirit, which God will provide when you ask.

It requires a positive attitude. Do not expect others' attitudes to change until yours does.

It requires faith that God will breathe on your blended family.

It requires prayer. God's breath and voice come as we spend time communicating with Him.

Becoming a solid blended family requires much from you, Mom and Dad. It is an investment into your future and your children's futures. The dividends are great!

Years ago, I was going through a painful divorce which I did not want. I cried out to God, and told Him that I was determined to see a blessing come from this divorce. Twelve years later, here

I am, writing a book with my best friend about the restoration and success that God has brought to us and to our children. Wow!

Do not give up! God never gives up on you!

No matter what has happened in your past, God has a plan to bring you into abundant life. Trust in God, your Father, and you will not be disappointed.

We pray that you and your blended family will become and will achieve all that God desires for you, which is more than you could ever imagine.

God, your Creator and Father, is breathtaking and life giving!

Hallelujah!

Healing Place Productions, Inc.

The vision for Healing Place Productions, Inc. was birthed out of the heart of Trinity Christian Center in Baton Rouge, Louisiana to be "A Healing Place for a Hurting World." This heart of our church to deliver God's love and healing power to Baton Rouge and throughout the world has resulted in tremendous church growth, increasing from 25 members in the first year to 1,200 in five years, and to 2,200 in seven years.

One of the major reasons for this growth has been the willingness of the Praise & Worship Team, led by Worship Pastor DeLynn Rizzo, to be open vessels as they have allowed God to use their artistic abilities to usher people into God's presence. It is in God's presence that people find healing for their hurting lives. The Team truly produces passionate praise and worship through an attitude that God is their "only" audience.

The Team's heart is to help other churches move to a new level in worship by creating an appreciation of the arts and bringing an openness to various styles of worship, and disregarding the number of people in the congregation.

Our Praise & Worship Team produced its first Worship CD entitled "Healing Place" in 1998. The Team will produce its second CD in 2000.

Healing Place Productions, Inc. has also developed a successful church leadership training program to raise up leaders in the local church to properly handle the great harvest that Trinity Christian Center has experienced.

Following is a list of resources available through Healing Place Productions, Inc.

Resources available through Healing Place Productions, Inc.:

Praise & Worship

"Healing Place", Praise and Worship CD $15.00
DeLynn Rizzo and Candace Austin, and the Healing Place Band and Choir

"Healing Place", Praise and Worship Cassette Tape $10.00
DeLynn Rizzo and Candace Austin, and the Healing Place Band and Choir

Audio Cassette Teachings

Life Works Investing in God's Principles for a Lifetime $20.00
            by Pastor Dino Rizzo   6 tape series

Joseph   Determination: How Big is Your Want To? $20.00
            by Pastor Dino Rizzo   4 tape series

David   A Man After God's Heart (Skilled, Passionate & Ordinary) $20.00
            by Pastor Dino Rizzo   6 tape series

When God Is In the Home $20.00
            by Pastor Wayne Austin   4 tape series

Books

God Breathes on Blended Families, by Moe and Paige Becnel $9.00

The Structure of Prayer, My Prayer Journal, by Pastor Mark Stermer $20.00

Other Resources

TGIS (Thank God I'm Single) Ministry & Singles Retreat Planning
Annual TGIS (Thank God I'm Single) Celebration
Annual Performing Arts Conference
Annual "Times of Refreshing" Pastors/ Leaders Conference
Nursery & Children's Ministry Planning
Student Ministry Planning
Men's Ministry Planning
Women's Ministry Planning
College Ministry Planning

If we can be of any service to you, please contact us at:

Healing Place Productions, Inc.
19202 Highland Rd.
Baton Rouge, LA 70809
Phone: 225-753-2273
Fax: 225-753-7175.
Email: info@healingplacechurch.org
Website: healingplacecchurch.org